DOC'S SURVIVAL RULES

DOC'S SURVIVAL RULES

James E. Palen, MD

Copyright © 2025 James E. Palen, MD.

All rights reserved. No part of this book may be reproduced, stored, or transmitted by any means—whether auditory, graphic, mechanical, or electronic—without written permission of both publisher and author, except in the case of brief excerpts used in critical articles and reviews. Unauthorized reproduction of any part of this work is illegal and is punishable by law.

ISBN: 979-8-89419-713-5 (sc)
ISBN: 979-8-89419-714-2 (hc)
ISBN: 979-8-89419-715-9 (e)

Because of the dynamic nature of the Internet, any web addresses or links contained in this book may have changed since publication and may no longer be valid. The views expressed in this work are solely those of the author and do not necessarily reflect the views of the publisher, and the publisher hereby disclaims any responsibility for them.

One Galleria Blvd., Suite 1900, Metairie, LA 70001
(504) 702-6708

CONTENTS

RULE 1: Every Night Takeoff is an Instrument Takeoff ...1

RULE 2: Never Hesitate to Declare an Emergency........7

RULE 3: Always Land with One Hour of Fuel in the Tanks 11

RULE 4: Never Leave the Ground with an Unexplained Issue.........................17

RULE 5: Never Hesitate to Ask for Clarification of a Clearance............................21

RULE 6: Never Hesitate to Abort a Landing 27

RULE 7: With Any Ice on the Aircraft, at Low Altitude, Do Not Extend Flaps 31

RULE 8: If One Engine Fails During a Multi-Engine Takeoff, Anticipate Imminent Failure of the Second Engine 37

RULE 9: During Night Landings, if the Runway Lights Suddenly Go Off, Make an Emergency Maximum Performance Climb 41

RULE 10: It's Time for a "Safety Pilot" 45

JUST A COUPLE ADDITIONAL THOUGHTS....................49

RULE 1

Every Night Takeoff is an Instrument Takeoff

> **Every night takeoff is an instrument takeoff.**

Takeoff is the most dangerous part of any flight. This is true because during this process, the aircraft is near a stall attitude, at a low airspeed, at a low altitude, with rapidly decreasing runway available. Loss of situational awareness can develop rapidly with devastating consequences.

Night takeoffs are virtually always a low-visibility situation once the aircraft rotates. Without visual cues, the pilot is left with only the input from the labyrinthine system and the sensation of acceleration and increased weight. As the aircraft accelerates and rotates, the inner ear presents the pilot with sensations that can easily be misinterpreted. For example, acceleration produces an input similar to that of a pitch up. Similarly, the sensation of increased weight mimics that of a climb. Forces on the aircraft, such as the gyroscopic effect of a spinning propeller, compound the situation. Unless the pilot refers to attitude instruments, a climbing turn, usually to the right, degrading into a diving turn can feel like a normal straight-ahead climb.

Pilots can find themselves in other low-visibility situations, where this same mindset should be routine. For example, low-lying clouds, haze, and fog can cause some terrain features to be misinterpreted as a horizon. A takeoff over water is another example of a time when it is easy to lose the horizon. Any one of these examples should prompt a pilot to monitor instruments. Instruments should also be monitored closely during any change in aircraft attitude or configuration and certainly upon entering IMC.

During any low-visibility takeoff, a well-trained pilot will always use the full length of the runway and monitor the instruments to attain a safe altitude while maintaining the appropriate attitude and heading. The pilot should be on the instruments until the aircraft is safely established straight and level, or in cruise climb, on course.

RULE 2

Never Hesitate to Declare an Emergency

> **Never hesitate to declare an emergency.**

I understand that low-time pilots and student pilots may be hesitant to declare an emergency. However, well-trained pilots with significant experience readily recognize that declaring an emergency is an invaluable tool for the pilot with a problem. Even what appears to be a relatively minor issue can rapidly degrade into a bold-face emergency. Once the pilot declares an emergency, air traffic controllers are able to provide an increased level of assistance and special handling that may not otherwise be available.

Declaring an emergency is never a mistake, but not doing so may well be.

Do not wait for permission to take action in an

emergency. Take action, notify ATC, and declare an emergency, in that order. For example, cabin pressurization concerns at flight level 250 is an emergency. The pilot should start to descend, then notify ATC that he/she has started to descend, declare an emergency, and describe the nature of the emergency. Then tell ATC what type of assistance you require.

During recurrent training, instructors should encourage pilots to declare an emergency at the first sign of trouble. This should become an integral part in managing any condition that can affect the safe conclusion of the flight, not just a boldface emergency.

Some pilots are hesitant to declare an emergency; this is a mistake. Pilots will never be criticized for declaring an emergency. There is a common misconception that declaring an emergency results in a significant amount of paperwork or critical scrutiny by the FAA. I can tell you from experience that this is not the case. Among the several times I have had occasion to declare an emergency, I have never been asked to file a written report. And on the rare occasion when I discussed the precipitating issue with an FAA representative, the person with whom I spoke was very polite, understanding, and helpful.

RULE 3

Always Land with One Hour
of Fuel in the Tanks

Always land with one hour of fuel in the tanks.

The rules don't require it, but this is my self-imposed rule. I monitor fuel status throughout flight, and if I find myself running short of this standard, I land short for fuel. I prefer to plan the fuel stop as soon as I know a stop will be required. This gives me more options as to when and where to stop. During pre-flight planning, I like to identify potential airports where fuel and other services will be available if required.

I like to use fuel from my auxiliary tanks at about one hour into the flight. This allows me to be sure that the tanks actually contain fuel and that the fuel is actually usable.

I remember flying on a very cold day when fuel in an auxiliary tank in the wing could not be used because of a frozen valve in the wing root. It's easy to see how challenging this could be flying in some remote areas and failing to recognize this problem early in the flight.

From many years of experience, I know unexpected changes can occur during the course of a flight that can make fuel quantity marginal. We've all experienced things like a change in the winds aloft, deviations for weather, aux tanks unreachable or inadvertently left empty, delayed engine leaning, or unexpected weather enroute or at our destination.

RULE 4

Never Leave the Ground with
an Unexplained Issue

Never leave the ground with an unexplained issue.

We as pilots are responsible for establishing the airworthy condition of our aircraft prior to takeoff. It is impossible to establish an airworthy condition if there is an unexplained issue. Taking an aircraft into the air with an unexplained issue is fraught with danger. Close to the ground is no place to have to diagnose and deal with even a minor problem, much less a serious one. Take-off roll is no place to ask, "What is making that noise?" or "Why is that light flashing?"

Call for an abort early. There is nothing shameful or embarrassing about calling for an abort. Remember, takeoff is the most dangerous part of any flight.

An unanticipated sound, vibration, or the "feel" of the controls can be the first indication of a developing serious problem. Personally, if there is an issue with the plane, I prefer to handle it on the ground rather than in the air.

RULE 5

Never Hesitate to
Ask for Clarification
of a Clearance

Never hesitate to ask for clarification of a clearance.

It is critical that you understand what is expected of you when you accept a clearance. Controllers rely on your compliance with the clearance you have accepted in handling traffic flow. Therefore, you must be sure you understand and can comply with every element of any clearance you accept. I do not consider it good practice to accept a clearance while taxiing unless there is a second pilot onboard.

Remember, a clearance is not a one-sided proposition. It's more like an agreement between you and air traffic control. You, as the pilot in command, have the right to accept or decline any clearance. However, once you have accepted a clearance, you are then bound by the terms of the clearance. You, as the pilot in command, should never accept a clearance with which you cannot comply or that would put your aircraft in jeopardy.

In the event you have accepted a clearance and then discovered you cannot comply or that complying would put your aircraft in jeopardy, you must notify ATC immediately. This will allow air traffic control to make appropriate adjustments in traffic flow in a timely manner so as to not put you's or any other aircraft in jeopardy.

RULE 6

Never Hesitate to
Abort a Landing

Never hesitate to abort a landing.

If an approach is not timely stabilized, a well-trained pilot will abort the landing and go around. It's much better to go around early than to wish you had late.

If any crew member is uncomfortable with the landing setup, the prudent thing to do is abort the landing, climb to a safe altitude, and discuss the issue.

Any crew member should be comfortable calling for a go-around. Short final is no place to discuss safety or operational issues. Whether flying single pilot or as a crew, anytime the stability of the approach becomes an issue, the landing should be aborted.

Aircraft in the skies today have more speed, complexity, and capability. All of these improvements are a good thing. However, they come at a price. It is easier to get behind the aircraft. In the event you find yourself getting behind the aircraft, consider slowing down, asking for a delaying vector or hold, and asking for help. Rushing the approach and landing setup can lead to mistakes. For example, "Three in the green?"

RULE 7

With Any Ice on the Aircraft, at Low Altitude, Do Not Extend Flaps

> **With any ice on the aircraft, at low altitude, do not extend flaps.**

In icing conditions, the tail of the aircraft will tend to accrue ice before the wings. It is difficult to determine how much ice may have actually formed on the tail. However, any ice on the tail will increase the potential for the tail to stall. And the weight of significant ice may result in an aft CG. When the tail stalls, the nose of the aircraft will drop, requiring a prompt response from the pilot. The required response in a tailplane stall is different from a stall of the wing in that an increase in pitch and a possible decrease in power will likely be required. If the CG has in fact moved aft, such a stall would be unrecoverable with devastating results. In any event, significant altitude can be lost.

With ice on the aircraft tail, extending flaps can precipitate a tailplane stall since the extended flaps further disrupt airflow over the tail. Flaps should be used with caution in icing conditions and should not be extended at low altitude, such as final approach, and never on short final.

RULE 8

If One Engine Fails During
a Multi-Engine Takeoff,
Anticipate Imminent
Failure of the
Second Engine

> **If one engine fails during a multi-engine takeoff, anticipate imminent failure of the second engine.**

What could cause an engine failure during takeoff? Well, certainly internal engine issues can, but oftentimes when there is an engine issue, the engine loses some power but does not just stop. However, fuel contamination or refueling a piston aircraft with jet fuel can cause sudden total engine failure. This could easily occur during or shortly after takeoff. What is more important in a twin-engine aircraft is that upon failure of one engine on takeoff, the second engine will likely fail shortly thereafter.

The pre-takeoff brief in a multi-engine aircraft should brief engine loss but also include planning for the loss of the second engine.

I would prefer to stay on the runway or abort the takeoff. This is one reason I recommend using the full length of a runway. But if aborting is not possible, the closest runway would be my choice. And I would attempt to remain VFR. Of course, every situation is different. This is why we do a takeoff brief.

I experienced this when flying out of Allegheny County Airport with contaminated fuel. After losing the right engine in the climb, we circled back to land on the nearest runway. We lost the second engine after landing while taxiing clear of the runway. My recommendation is: declare an emergency, do not allow yourself to be vectored away from the airport, and insist on the nearest runway.

RULE 9

During Night Landings, if the Runway Lights Suddenly Go Off, Make an Emergency Maximum Performance Climb

> **During night landings, if the runway lights suddenly go off, make an emergency maximum performance climb.**

When landing at night, if the runway's lights suddenly go out, one of two things has happened. Either the runway lights have indeed timed out or been switched off, or the aircraft has flown behind an obstruction like terrain, foliage, or some man-made structure.

The safest course for the pilot and the aircraft is an immediate maximum performance climb to a safe altitude. The pilot can then evaluate the situation in a safe setting.

Altitude and distance are hard to judge with any degree of accuracy at night. I find it best to use VASA lights and glide slope whenever these are available. If these aids are not available, I recommend entering a standard traffic pattern. This provides the best chance for a stabilized final approach.

RULE 10

It's Time for a "Safety Pilot"

It's time for a "Safety Pilot"

With challenging weather, unfamiliar aircraft or avionics, advancing age, or decreasing proficiency, it's time for a safety pilot.

I believe that a safety pilot is always a good idea. But in challenging situations, I consider it essential. It is prudent to know the flight instructors in your area and the names of pilots who have the ability to act as safety pilot. Over the years, I have flown a number of times as a safety pilot for other pilots.

As I have gotten older, now in my eighties, I no longer fly with passengers without a safety pilot. Though I still maintain my medical and flight instructor rating and do recurrent training, the thought of leaving my wife or other friends or family in a plane with me disabled leaves me very uncomfortable. I actually find flying as a crew less stressful and more enjoyable.

JUST A COUPLE ADDITIONAL THOUGHTS

Situational Awareness

Sometimes it's easy to get so focused on an issue that we lose track of time and the broader picture around us. In an aircraft, the picture is in a constant state of flux. This rapidly changing environment can result in the pilot getting behind the aircraft. It is critical that the pilot stays ahead of the aircraft. If you find yourself getting behind, slow down, request a hold, and ask for assistance. Do not let yourself be rushed or overwhelmed.

Accident Chain

We all know that accidents are seldom the result of a single event or decision. Accidents are most often the result of a series of relatively benign events or decisions. For example, flying fatigued, single pilot, into bad weather, in an aircraft just out of maintenance, at night, into an unfamiliar airport. Any one of these elements presents some concern. But as additional elements are added, the risk of an accident increases. When planning a flight, look for the possibility of an accident chain developing, and consider how you can mitigate the risk.

ABOUT THE AUTHOR

Back in 1959, it was a Cessna 150 that started the whole thing. Like many young people I began flying for fun with no idea how aviation would impact my life. Some years later, after medical school, I began a serious program to improve my flying skills. First was multi-engine and instrument training in a Cessna 310K. Over the subsequent years, I had a number of different aircraft, finally settling on the Cessna 421C Golden Eagle.

As our children became interested in flying, a CFII seemed prudent. Later, I added the ATP rating.

I have been an FAA-designated senior aviation medical examiner since the mid-1970s. And in 2001, I retired from the USAF as a colonel, command flight surgeon IMA, at Air Education Training Command. I must give a great deal of credit for my approach to aviation and flying skills to the many air force pilots with whom I have shared the cockpit.

My oldest son and I continue the practice of family medicine and aerospace medicine, providing care for our patients and the many pilots who rely on our service. I do, however, take plenty of time with Shirley, my wife, and our children, grandchildren, and some great-grandchildren. And of course, our many friends.

Thank you for your time. Fly smart and fly safe.

James E. Palen, MD, AAFP, ABFM
Col. USAF MC CFS (Ret.)
Senior Aviation Medical Examiner
ATP MEL, Com SEL, CFII, MEL, SEL

www.ingramcontent.com/pod-product-compliance
Lightning Source LLC
LaVergne TN
LVHW070939070526
838199LV00035B/654